FRESH HEARTS

THAT FAILED THREE THOUSAND YEARS AGO;

WITH

OTHER THINGS

BY THE AUTHOR OF

"THE NEW PRIEST IN CONCEPTION BAY."

BOSTON:
TICKNOR AND FIELDS.
M DCCC LX.

RIVERSIDE, CAMBRIDGE:
PRINTED BY H. O. HOUGHTON AND COMPANY.

Having from childhood met, now and then, and listened to the Muse of Numbers, the writer offers here a few of the few things that he has learned, at different times, from her, and hopes that they may not be thought too many.

Several of the pieces in this book, he does not count as poetry; they are here for their religious character; some, he believes to have some worth as poetry.

Lest the dates, put to most of them, should be thought to have been occasioned by a conceit or affectation, it is right to say that they are owing to a friend's discovery of a remarkable chance-likeness between one of these, printed years ago, and a recent poem in a Magazine. One being dated, some others, at least, must be so; and in the end, most of these pieces have had the time at which they were written, given, after them. The general reader will be kind enough to pass over these dates as harmless; some friends may even find a slight interest in them.

March, 1860.

CONTENTS.

ERRATUM.

In correcting the press, a mistake, in the piece entitled "The Little Years," p. 14, 3d line of verse 1, was overlooked. Please read *caught* instead of *met.*

AN ANTHEM-CAROL FOR CHRISTMAS.

Out of highest heaven dropping,
Like tinkling rain upon the sea
Came sweet music, swelling, stopping;
'T was the angels' symphony.
"Glory be to God, on high!"
Ran like lightning round the sky:
Then, like rain-drops fell agen
"Peace on earth, good-will to men!"

1846.

FRESH HEARTS THAT FAILED THREE THOUSAND YEARS AGO.

THIS little tragedy shaped itself in my mind from the suggestion of two or three words in a note to a Greek Author, as I remembered them, afterwards; a poem 'by a boy' (without a name) was mentioned as having come down from earlier times.

FRESH HEARTS

THAT FAILED THREE THOUSAND YEARS AGO.

I.

A YOUTH lay near the fair gulf's * fringéd shore ;
The noise of Corinth scarcely came so far ;
But landward sounds, that, when the day is o'er,
Tell where blest homes and ended labors are.
On the broad bay, behind,
Lugged by the lazy wind,
A freighted ship drew on, towards the evening-star.

II.

The little waters, as the daylight waned,
Lagged up the beach, prattling with shell and stone ;

* Of Corinth.

The eastern sky was all with sunset stained,
Where the two heads of that great mountain* shone.
Lower, each vale and glade
Drew in, to deeper shade,
The eye of him that gazed from that far shore alone.

III.

Still lay, bright-hued, in air, both far and wide,
All crumbled rays the sun had thrown away;
And, floating thick on the night's dewy tide,
Came smells more sweet than scents of burning day;
And then a voice, — as fair
As all the best things there, —
Scarce startling him; old, gentle, sweet, and sad as
they: —

IV.

" Thou musest of the gifts that, yonder, wait
Those whom the Gods do choose with far-off ken:
Castalia's spell,† and the rich, dreamy freight
Laid on Sleep's shore,‡ for favored sons of men.

* Mount Parnassus.

† Whoever drank of the water, might drink the divine spirit also.

‡ He that slept upon Parnassus, in waking found his mind possessed by poetic inspiration, or was possessed by madness.

I sought one sacred gift:—
Ah! Time's waves, strong and swift,
Have swept bright looks and hopes, that made my world glad, then.

V.

"Beside a pool, where, still, two olives meet,
Three-score years since, some Delphian * children played:
We built our little mole and launched our fleet,
And then along the rippling margin strayed
Watching the voyage o'er,
Till, at the farther shore,
Our galleys, one by one, on the safe strand were laid.

VI.

"Mine, ever mine, was foremost in the race,
Till, tired, our little maidens sat them down,
Whispered apart,—then sang:—one, with bright face,
Said, 'Let our poet wear a Pythian crown!'

* The city of Delphi, where was the great temple of Apollo, stood upon the mountain, a mile or more from the foot.

They wove the dark-leaved beech,
Each helping, hindering each,
Then, in child's triumph, all turned homeward to
the town.

VII.

"On huge Parnassus hung a wondrous cloud, —
We children marked it, — much like yon fair show;
Again Alcestis spoke, but scarce aloud,
'At times the mighty Shades do gather so.
(So did my mother say;)
They come not in the day,
But in still night, to walk the high woods to and
fro.'

VIII.

"Shades of the great old Greeks and Barbarous
men,
Whoe'er on earth had loosed some mighty song:
At times by night they wandered here, and then
What poet found the haunt of the dread throng
On that far mountain-height,
Ere dawn was lost in light,
That once, plucked fadeless flowers that to their realm
belong.

IX.

"My heart beat quickly, as we gazed and walked,
For they had all praised my own childish rhyme;
Evadne, too, my sister, while we talked,
Turned her full eyes, as if I, child, might climb
Up to that haunted land;
Alcestis pressed my hand
As if she felt my heart throb at the very time.

X.

"I lost our Pythian garland in the road,
While we walked thoughtfully, and sometimes spake.
The wondrous cloud with the last sunlight glowed,
As yon cloud lately: — might not we awake, —
We three, — from early rest,
And on the mountain's breast,
Climb with fresh, hopeful hearts, high ere the day
could break?

XI.

"Out of glad day, through the fair porch of eve,
Our playmates passed into the halls of sleep.
I listened long, for the great town to leave
Its noise and watchfulness, and long rest keep.

Then faltered forth, to gain
The great god's awful fane,
Scared by each far, lone cry, and the far, conscious
deep.

XII.

"I shrank before the columns cloaked with shade,
And, shuddering, felt a fanning of great wings:
I dared not that chill presence to invade,
Dim with dread forms of gods and godlike kings.
I gasped my childish prayer:
I had no garland there
To offer, as men vow their gifts and glorious things.

XIII.

"Ere that fair night had reached her highest bound,
We met and grasped each other's trembling hand;
With faltering whispers scaled the fearful ground,
Three children where dread rocks and huge trees
stand.
On high the broad moon rolled;
And her rays, white and cold,
From darkness, here and there, scarce won the doubt-
ful land.

XIV.

"We kept a torrent's course, and, trembling still,
Went on and on, starting and stopping oft:
Sometimes we sat and wept, as children will,
And my cheek felt Evadne's, wet and soft:
'Home!' she would gently say,
'Nay!' said Alcestis, 'nay!'
And still we clambered on, through the dread woods,
aloft.

XV.

"Hours, hours went on, and cold and darkness grew:
Still, weary and afraid, we clambered fast,
And dawn began to gray the night's deep blue:
We gained the upper woods! — The way was past!
Now need we only seek
Where the two echoes speak,
Above, below, at once, to find the flowers that last.

XVI.

"Our voices faltered, when we strove to sing:
We feared the trees, the rocks, the quivering gloom:
At length we dared our little hymn to fling
Through the thin air, where shadowy horrors loom.

Lo! at the earliest sound,
The mystic spot was found,
And there a high, smooth cliff, crowned with undying bloom.

XVII.

" Great characters upon the rock's high face
Slowly we saw, in the dim dawning light;
'MEN THAT WERE MAKERS,' * far up we could trace,
And then their names that had the Maker's might;
We thought not what great hand
Had made those names to stand:
We thought that at the foot a boy's name we might write.

XVIII.

" So, with weak hand, I sought to print the stone,
The little maidens sitting at my side.
'First,' said Alcestis, 'make the flowers thine own!'
'Nay,' said Evadne, with a sister's pride,
'Let our young poet's name
Stand on this roll of fame!'
So I, with hurrying hand, my weary labor plied.

* 'ἌΝΔΡΕΣ ΠΟΙΗΤΑΙ·' it may be read.

XIX.

" Slowly the dawning grew, and slowly I
Now wrought, now rested ; but Alcestis still
Said, ' Gather first the blooms that hang on high !
Day will be here ere thou this task fulfil :
Yon peak sees it afar,
And yonder shrinking star ;
First gain the fadeless flowers, then work here at
thy will.'

XX.

" Four letters rudely in the stone were wrought,
And could be read, ' A Boy,' * but yet no name.
' See,' said Alcestis, ' how the peak has caught
Already daylight : soon 't will be a-flame.
It is not yet too late !
Mount where the bright flowers wait :
Flowers that, when thou art dead, will ever be the
same ! '

XXI.

" I tried the cliff, and climbed : my hands were sore,
And I was tired : yet I strained up the height.
The little maidens shouted, ' Yet once more ! '

* 'ΠΑΙΣ·' — but as yet no name, *it may be read.*

I tried: I tried: I could not reach them quite.
And ah! behold on high,
Ah! all across the sky,
The day was come, at last, and *dawn was lost in light.*

XXII.

"My tears burst forth: in vain my sister said,
'They are still there!'—I knew it was in vain.
It was too late.—Alcestis hung her head.
Sadly I came down to the earth, again.
'Home!' said Alcestis, now:
Evadne kissed my brow;
And, by our torrent's course, we toiled down to the plain."

The little waters trickled down the beach,
And landward sounds fell, faintly, to their rest.
The dews were heavy, and that sad, soft speech
Had ceased, just when the ear had liked it best.
The young man was alone,
And great cool night was thrown
Over wide earth and sea, from far east to far west.

1858.

THE DAYS OF SIN.

Oh mournful, mournful time!
  I prayed: but sin was there:
  Sin crept upon my prayer,
And made my prayer a crime!

I prayed, and prayed again:
  But sin was in it still!
  It throttled my weak will;
I struggled — but in vain.

I burned by day and night,
  I feared that fire of sin —
  Its covering seemed so thin —
Would show to others' sight!

My daily work I did, —
  I talked of Heaven and Hell,
  Full often and full well —
But ah! what woe I hid!

It seemed as if my fate
  Were up: in Satan's mesh —
  A damnéd soul in flesh —
I lived beyond my date.

Christ's life in me seemed lost!
  Where was the promise now,
  Sealed to me when my brow
In his bless'd sign was cross'd?

I strove to fly from me;
  Always it was the same;
  Hell was where'er I came;
God's wrath I could not flee.

Such life I loathed to keep,
  But could I dare to die?
  Heaven's walls so hopeless high,
And Hell a soundless deep?

My heart aye told me well
  I gave myself away,

To be the Devil's prey —
By my own hand I fell.

I struggled once for all;
God's altar — there I prayed;
And bitter cry I made
Behind my closet wall.

A change began to be!
I felt the Breath of Life!
For Heaven and Hell was strife:
I struggled, and was free!

Ah! now the strife was done,
I sought the Flesh and Blood:
I ate Salvation's food;
My soul to Christ was won.

February 10, 1847.

THE LITTLE YEARS.

A SONG FOR THE ELDER GRADUATES.

THESE years! These years! These naughty years
Once they were pretty things:
Their fairy foot-falls met our ears,
Our eyes their glancing wings.
They flitted by our school-boy way;
We chased the little imps at play.

We knew them, soon, for tricksy elves;
They brought the college gown;
With thoughtful books filled up our shelves,
Darkened our lips with down:
Played with our throat, and lo! the tone
Of manhood had become our own.

They smiling stretched our childish size;
Their soft hands trimmed our hair;
Cast the deep thought within our eyes
And left it glowing there:

Sang songs of hope in college-halls,
Bright fancies drew upon the walls.

They flashed upon us love's bright gem;
They showed us gleams of fame;
Stout-hearted work we learned from them,
And honor more than name:
And so they came and went away,
We said not go: we said not stay.

But one sweet day, when quiet skies
And still leaves brought me thought,
When hazy hills drew forth my eyes,
And woods with deep shade fraught,
That day I carelessly found out
What work these elves had been about.

Alas! Those little rogues, the years,
Had fooled me many a day;
Plucked half the locks above my ears,
And tinged the rest all gray.
They'd left me wrinkles, great and small:—
I fear that they have tricked us all.

Well, — give the little years their way;
Think, speak, and act the while:
Lift up the bare front to the day,
And make their wrinkles smile:
They mould the noblest living head;
They carve the best tomb for the dead.

July 20, 1858.

[A song ought to be capable of being sung: but, somehow, the author of this has just fitted it, apparently, *carere vate sacro*, — to go without its melody. He has been informed of several composers (whose touch was an honor to it) that have tried to set it to music, and have not been satisfied with the result.]

TURNING LOVE AWAY.

(LONG YEARS AGO.)

O LOVE, go forth! I brought thee here
For that I heard thee sing one day
When thou wast in the grass at play:
That song of one that was too dear.
O Love! — O Love! — I could not bear
To listen by the wayside there;
I longed to hear thee sing, somewhere
Where no one else was near.

Rememberest thou, my little guest?
In bearing thee, (thy pretty wing
Blinding my eyes, thou roguish thing!)
I wandered where my feet knew best.
She laid on thee one timid touch,
But oh! that little was so much,
The arrows in thy careless clutch
Stung all my open breast.

How bright the earth was, that glad time!
How sweetly breathed the evening air;
It seemed her breath was everywhere,
And ours became a fairy clime.
The sky hung all in gold and red;
The flowers all vied their scents to shed;
The ground seemed loving to my tread;
All sounds, that eve, did chime.

I gave thee but one only task:
To go as my true messenger,
And bring sweet words again from her,
The work thyself didst ask:
Until that day between us two
Thou broughtest lies; we thought them true,
So well our cunning traitor knew
His young, false face to mask.

I must shut up thy little room!—
Ah! o'er its yet unhardened wall
Thine arrow traced her name, and all
Her look, except her own fresh bloom!—

I could not come here but to weep:
Here was thy little couch to sleep;
These walls thy useless work will keep;
But this shall be a tomb.

Let me forget that lying tongue!
Ah, what a price its falsehood cost,
When once, was once forever, lost! —
Yet sleep that loss, lost things among!
For such this world makes no amends.
We drew apart and chose new friends:
So many a short, bright story ends,
Where two young hearts were wrung.

A WALK AMONG MEMORY'S GRAVES.

I.

Graves of the silent dead,
Ye echo to the tread
Of a lone, mourning man:
They were my friends of yore;
Sweet company they bore
To me when life began.

II.

I wander here, alone,
To seek if faithful stone
Is set by every grave;
And to call up again
Thoughts, cherished not in vain,
They to my young soul gave.

III.

Yours first I call, dear Hopes,
Seen on the sunny slopes,

Where as a child I lay;
Or that by winding brook,
My loitering steps o'ertook,
In the long summer day.

IV.

There was no sound of man;
My free soul forward ran
Among the coming years.
I felt the breath of fame:
I heard aloud my name:
My eyes were nigh to tears.

V.

Glad Hopes! Ye gave me then
What long, late toil to men
Brings only withering:
I plucked with childish gripe,
The fruit ere it was ripe;
But it was mine in spring.

VI.

Sweet, sweet, sad Hopes! what now
Is left upon the bough,

Of flower, or fruit, or leaf?
And yet, why mourn, if ye
So early gave to me
Thoughts, fair and bright, though brief?

VII.

Feelings of childhood's time,
That stretched about to climb
On all that stood around!
Whose twining grasp was laid,
In sunshine and in shade,
Tireless on all it found,—

VIII.

Whose hold was often flung
From that whereon ye clung,
Yet would not long be free;
By your fond instinct taught
I thought (true childhood's thought)
That all were kin to me.

IX.

Amid the boys' loud band
I seem again to stand;

Again quick-voiced and glad;
Feelings more great and strong
Than to child's sports belong
In those young days we had:

X.

The swell, ere storms begin,
When huge waves tumble in
And fill the little bay;
So from life's vexéd sea,
The strong, deep swell knew we,
In childhood's peaceful day.

XI.

That human brotherhood,
Mingling in every mood,
Made this our life so great,
The mystic, awful bond
Still urged me forth beyond
Myself, to feel my fate:

XII.

One of so many more,
Whom life was laid before

Full of mysterious things;
Where every human soul,
To the great common whole,
Its lore and insight brings.

XIII.

I look once more to see,
As at the chestnut tree
Where the far voices died,
The pleasant thoughts that played
Beneath that pleasant shade,
In troops on every side.

XIV.

Then youth came sailing o'er,
Fairer than all before,
Broad-sailed and deeply-fraught.
Love! Hope! Ambition! you
Mastered the lithe, strong crew.—
Love?—Hope?—Ambition?—Naught!

XV.

Yet, if they were but vain,
They come no more again

To make me loiter here:
The work that God has set,
It has the long days, yet,
And brightest of the year.

XVI.

Still has my chief work been
Rather to make me clean
As he must be that will
Go forth 'mid thronging men
And stretch his forward ken
Onward and upward, still.

* * * * * *

XVII.

No more, no more I call!
Cool, solemn shadows fall
Down on my open mind!
For this I wandered here—
For this I called you near,
Thoughts of things long resigned;

XVIII.

They will be raised one day,
And throng about the way

Of the old dying man;
Hopes, feelings, joys that smiled
Upon him when a child,
And o'er the bright scenes ran.

XIX.

Children in summer's eve,
Do pluck the old man's sleeve
And clamber up his knee;
Or draw him by the hand
To where their playthings stand,
Or their sweet sports to see.

XX.

Thus will these come, once more,
To lead him gently o'er
The scenes loved long ago;
And in his eldest days,
All childhood's long left ways
Make him again to know.

July, 1846.

[One stanza was put in and the neighboring parts adjusted to it in 1860.]

THE PAINTER'S PROBATION.

PART FIRST.

THERE comes in life a frequent hour,
When the full voice of Fate
Calls with a dread, mysterious power
On those who should be great:
To warn them that a mighty dower
Somewhere for them doth wait.
For somewhere, in the long, long train
That marches down through Time,
Working out human nature's gain,
Its glory or its crime,
For each a station doth remain:
With power to do or to refrain,
A humble or sublime.
And they whom God hath breathed upon
And gifted, from their birth,
With lofty powers to labor on
The labor of this earth,
For them, amid the swelling crowd,

An office is assigned
With mighty influence endowed;
And unto them Fate calleth, loud,
In the first-opening mind.
Again, again, through shine or cloud,
Her words come, as the wind.
Alas! how many, downward bowed,
Their birthright have resigned!
O God! How much of great and good,
How much of fearful sin,
Were gained, or gallantly withstood,
If these their place would win!

There hung upon the chamber-wall
The fancies he had wrought:
All that his soul had power to call,
Out of the shapes that shadow all,
Into his burning thought.
The hopes that gladdened early years
Had left their colors there,
And shades were there, that early fears
Had taught his art to wear:
Alternate smiles, alternate tears,

(So that young life to thought appears,)
Each memory had its share.
But in the dark and in the bright, —
Colored by joy or pain, —
Something was wanting to his sight :
The utmost all were vain.
Sweet strains of music from old days
Murmured about his soul,
And Memory's deep, golden haze,
An atmosphere of mingled rays,
O'er his wide thought would roll,
While airs, like summer wind that plays,
Would gently fan the whole.
Oh ! at such seasons, when he felt
As if his spirit, free
From the close body's narrow belt,
Swelled towards Divinity,
And pure and strong and living grew,
As when at first it came
From Him that sent it forth to do
Deeds that should earn a name,
Or, nameless, bear a blessing through
The paths of this world's shame,

Oh! why, when God himself inspired
Those raptured hours of thought,
The very seasons oft desired,
Why has he yet in vain retired,
And still no trophy brought,
Though, by a transient impulse fired,
Again he strove and wrought?
He saw the scene: he felt the force;
He started forth to do!
But no! the streamlet from its source
Bears flowers of every hue
Wrapped in their seeds; and, in its course,
It strews and plants them too:
But time, and place, and God's own smile
Must meet together, or long while
Unfruitful they must lie,
Ere they will show again the scene
From which they came, and which has been
Painted in many-colored sheen
Beneath another sky.
Thus all were vain: he could not find
Within his utmost power,
That form that floated in his mind,

Not indistinct, though not defined,
Leaving a memory behind,
Like tints at sunset hour.
His gleaming eye had caught its light,
His cheek had felt its glow;
And dreamily before his sight,
In the rapt visions of the night,
That fancy-form would go;
And when his spirit felt its might,
That form he seemed to know.
In the wild agony of prayer
His trembling hand had tried
To fix the fleeting figure there;
And he had sought in mad despair
The power that was denied.
All Beauty and all Holiness, —
(Alas! there mingled Sin,) —
Howe'er combined, could not express
That form he sought to win.
There was the blue of changeless Truth:
There was Love's burning red;
The golden-glowing Hope of Youth
Its yellow glory spread:

Oh, pure! oh, bright! oh, heavenly deep!
There seemed God's Light within,
And wings of angels seemed to sweep
The breathing words: but shades did creep
O'er all: there mingled Sin!
That chill, chill wind from o'er the graves
And from the cold, damp tomb,
That wind that frosts the hair it waves,
And pales the cheek's fresh bloom;
The bitter wind that we must face
As down life's hill we go apace,
And evening spreads its gloom; —
He felt its first cold-creeping breath,
And saw afar, in mist, the vast, dim shape of
Death.

Come down, O night of dreamless sleep!
Come to this sad, sad room:
This working will and spirit steep
In silence, not in gloom.
Be thou, O night of needed rest,
A calm, clear night of peace,
Wherein the voice of heavenly guest

Can sing his gentle soothings best,
That make earth's struggles cease;
And, in the shut and darkened mind,
Leave sweetest lingering notes behind,
That shall the calm increase,
Until with waking prayer they find,
As with a breath of morning wind,
A happy, fit release.
And ye, O flowers of earnest Thought,
That in his mind grew bright,
With fresher perfume shall be fraught
And fairer robes, of spirits caught,
Cast down in peaceful night.

1838 and 1846.

END OF PART FIRST.

THAT DEAD.

Is he gone? Oh! Is he gone?
And does the world still travel on,
Heedless of his loss,
Like a freighted ship, at sea,
Ploughing on, though there may be
One that perished suddenly,
In the deep, like dross?

He is dead: yes, he is dead:
Bands of earth bind down his head,
Bands of earth his feet.
They that stood and saw him die
Brushed the salt tear from the eye,
And they that wrapped him, by and by,
In his winding-sheet.

He was one that had high thought
In the mind-rooms where he wrought
For all others' sake;

And had looked along the way,
Where the halting-places lay,
Where, from every weary day,
He his rest would take.

December, 1846.

THE CHRIST FORGOTTEN IN OUR DAYS.

"Though He was rich, yet, for our sakes, He became poor. How hardly shall they that have riches enter into the kingdom of God! — The cares of this life, and the deceitfulness of riches choke the Word, and it becometh unfruitful. — Lay not up for yourselves treasures upon earth. — Take no thought for the morrow."

Christ in a wretched place was born,
Nor owned his very grave;
He lived both homeless and forlorn, —
His fellows such as rich men scorn, —
And ate what beggars gave.

And when the Lord of Life became
Poor, and of none esteem,
He bade his followers do the same;
For Him to choose a life of shame;
Earth's goods a curse to deem.

The poor He blessed, and opened wide
The kingdom to their feet;
And bade the rich man go divide
The wealth whereon he built his pride,
And give the poor to eat.

Not otherwise might he be made
Christ's brother and God's son;
For how could one in pomp arrayed
The family of Christ invade,
Where wealth and pomp was none?

Christ's brethren,—oh! what seraphim
Cared less for earthly good!
The rich, bright world to them was dim;
They marched along with Prayer and Hymn,
And left it, where it stood.

If in the Kingdom's early day,
Men gave up earth for Heaven,
If lands and wealth they gave away,
If dainty food and rich array,—
If all for Christ was given,

Then how unlike God's humble Son
Are they who bear his name!
In rich apparel every one,
No worldly good they care to shun:
Are those and these the same?

The rich, — the rich are everywhere ;
These fill the Temple too,
And scantly give the poor a share
To whom Christ said YE BLESSED ARE :
God's kingdom is for you.

O rich men ! who do claim to be
The followers of the Lamb,
What, what are you, and what was He ?
Is not His name a mockery ?
Is not your faith a sham ?

I see your houses cedar-lined :
Ye feed each earthborn lust
For food, for gems, for gold refined,
For every pleasure that can bind
The spirit down to dust.

What single thing that wealth can buy
Do ye, for Christ, forget ?
To BEAR THY CROSS, THYSELF DENY, —
Know ye these words ? Were they to die,
Or are they living yet ?

Has Christ taught you another way,
The Fathers never knew,
To live well here, and live for aye?
To have the riches earth can pay,
And those hereafter too?

And yet ye cant of serving God
And giving to his poor,
Who go unfed, unclothed, unshod,
And underneath the heavy sod
First find a sleep secure.

O men well clothed, and warmed, and filled
While God's poor children fast,
The very churches that ye build
And deck with pomp and carve and gild
Will judge you at the last.

WHERE ARE MY POOR, Christ still demands, —
To whom the Gospel came?
This costly offering at your hands
Is to yourselves, and only stands
A monument of shame.

GIVE TO MY POOR! give much: give all,
If nothing less will do;
They that at first obeyed the call,
Were fain to let earth's riches fall:
Shall I ask less of you?

June, 1849.

THE CRY OF THE WRONGED.

The allusion, in the fourth stanza, to the startling emptiness of the hovel from which one of those poor people, who are just suffered to live in this world, has gone to another, will be recognized in full force by any one who has, even once in his life, looked in upon such a sight. I have seen, on untwisting the string from the nail and pushing open the crazy door, literally almost no relics but the handful of ashes upon the hearth, and the little heap of dust, laid out upon the bench, waiting to be given back to the earth from which it was taken. God help our poor brethren!

Brother, I am only dust:
Wherefore wilt thou be unjust?
Wherefore shake my humble trust
In our God, my brother?
There is yet but little day
That together we shall stay:
Wherefore jostle me away?
Love we one another.

I have but this little spot:
From my poor need snatch it not:
It is all that I have got
Of this hard world's giving.

Is there not a room for me,
Among all God made to be,
Where to gather, manfully,
Yet with toil my living?

God has given light and air:
Grudge not thou my little share;
Lo! it cometh everywhere,
We may share together.
God, Himself, has set me here,
And, with many a bitter tear,
I have struggled many a year
Of rough and wintry weather.

Let me work, — I ask no more, —
Till my stint is labored o'er.
I can never lay up store;
None this world will send me.
When I go, if men look there,
They will find my place all bare;
Nothing but the light and air,
God was good to lend me.

Brother, look at me again:
Toil has given me many a stain,
Toil has swollen every vein,
Yet I am thy brother.
I am man, as well as thou,
And our Lord has crossed my brow,
Calling me God's child, and how
Wilt thou call me other?

Let me stay until He call:
Let me stay till evening fall,
If so long I must be thrall,
My hard labor plying.
When thou comest to take share
In my cold bed, thou wilt there
Grant my claim, and little care
Near the poor man lying.

December, 1846.

A CHRISTMAS SERMON.

On the glorious Birthday morning,
All the church is dressed in green ;
Loud are heard the holy anthems,
Sweetest prayers go up between.

He that lay in lowly manger,
Now is known as Heaven's King ;
What but angels sang, aforetime,
Now have men been taught to sing :

"God have glory, in the highest :
Peace on earth, good-will towards men :
Over all the tide of ages,
Ever now as it was then."

After prayers and chant all ended,
Then the priest begins to preach :
In God's name he speaketh plainly,
For God's sake he loveth each.

" Lo ! " he saith, " the Lord of Glory,
Born and cradled in a stall !
Sure He had but scanty welcome,
Seeing He was Lord of all.

" Yet, in sooth, He sought no other,
Nor to earth for homage came;
Here He took the form of servant ;
Here He bared the cheek to shame.

" Not of this world was His kingdom :
He lived not at monarch's cost :
He sought not the known and honored,
But He came to seek the lost :

" Lost from out the world's long annals,
For they came of humble kin :
Lost from out the Book of Heaven,
For their life was led in sin.

" Thus the poor, and thus the sinner,
Found the Lord beside their door :
Heard His blessed words of comfort,
Such as no man spake before.

"Let our thoughts, this day, my brethren,
Seek the poor, by men forgot;
Whom the holy Christ remembered,
Coming here to share their lot.

"This world hath its rich and needy:
This world hath its high and low:
On the one side, pomp and worship;
On the other, toil and woe.

"Not forever shall we struggle
With the trials of this state:
To be poor, and yet be thankful;
To be lowly-willed, if great.

"Yet a little, and the Judgment:
Then we change for good or ill:
Rich or poor shall enter heaven,
As they did the Father's will.

"To be rich we may not covet,
Ye have heard the Saviour say:
And He chose the lowest station
When He came to earth this day.

"He has told us of His kingdom,
Hardly shall the rich go in;
Though the best that this world offers, —
Power and glory, — wealth may win.

"I will tell a simple story:
Every day it falleth true;
Jesu grant you all, my brethren,
That it be not so of you.

"See you there how Dives sitteth,
Richly clad, at dainty fare?
Many servants make obeisance,
Many guests sit humbly there.

"Now one cometh, speaking softly,
'Lazarus is at the gate:
Waiting, in full mournful fashion,
That his welcome cometh late.

"'For he meekly claimeth kindred,
Though he is of low degree.'
Heed the rich man, now, my brethren;
Scornful answer maketh he:

" 'Lazarus? I know no beggars,
And my kin bear no such name:
Yet these poor folk have their kindred;
Bid him go from whence he came.'

" 'Good my lord, the dogs are licking,
In mere ruth, his running sore;
He is modest, and he claimeth
But the crumbs from off thy floor.'

" 'Prating varlet!' said the rich man,
'Now what idle knaves have I!
Was there none to bid this beggar
Choose a fitter place to die?'

" He forgot that in God's heaven,
Righteous poor shall have their share:
And he thrust him from the threshold,
Caring nought how he might fare.

" So the servants laid the beggar
Just before another's gate;
Coming back, with due obeisance,
At their master's side to wait.

" Soon the poor man died, full godly,
And with saints he went to dwell:
Next the rich man died, and, after,
Lifted up his eyes in hell ;

" And afar he saw the poor man,
As he lay in Abraham's breast ;
And, from out his place of torment,
Prayed towards that blissful rest.

" 'T was but for a drop of water :
Yet his boon he could not win :
God had set a gulf, forever,
'Twixt the two that were not kin.

" For the words of dreadful judgment,
Christ hath told us what they be :
'I was hungry, sick, and naked,
And ye had no care of me.'

" Then shall they make forward answer,
That on earth had Him forgot :
'Lord, when saw we Thee an-hungered,
Sick, and naked, and cared not ?'

"Christ shall say, 'These poor and wretched,
Whose meek claim ye put aside,
I do own them as my brethren,
And in them was I denied.

"'When ye saw me not, nor heard me,
It was I put up the claim:
I lay pining at the threshold,
For they sought you in my name.'

"Let us, then, confess Christ's brother,
Lest we claim another kin:
Then, before the gate of heaven,
He shall bid us enter in.

"Glory, worship, love, and service,
To the blessed One in Three:
As it was in the beginning,
Is, and evermore shall be!"

THE BISHOP BOUND.

[After a missionary bishop had been sent out to Jerusalem, by the English Church, a great storm was raised in England, because he suffered some members of the superstitious and decrepid Eastern Church, in the midst of which he stood, to learn the Gospel of him.]

"Necessity is laid upon me."

Ye tell me that I must not preach
The Gospel to these men,
And if it struggles up to speech,
Must choke it down — and then? —

I may stand here, with dimming eyes,
And watch the world abroad;
For what? — Lest they, in any wise,
Should catch the truth of God.

They have "Most Holy Lords" to reign
Where poor Apostles wrought:
Shall "Right Divine" God's work restrain
And bring His Faith to nought?

Can tapers, robes, and painted saints,
And chant of old-time words
Save, more than flowers that sunlight paints,
Or out-door song of birds ?

If living faith in God's own Son
Alone true life can give,
Shall I undo what God has done,
Nor bid these dead men live ?

The winds are His, as well as I,
And, as their quick feet flit,
They will not let the message die
But men shall hear of it.

Could ye stand by me in my need,
When the last Judge is set,
And all is done, of human deed,
But not accounted, yet ?

Oh, no ! this breath I breathe, of air,
And shape in words, to-day,
Must preach His Gospel everywhere,
Or woe is mine for aye.

January 15, 1854.

A COMMUNING WITH GOD

BEFORE ENTERING INTO HOLY ORDERS.

WHAT hands will now be laid upon me, Lord?
Whose spirit breathed, whose blessed influence given?
By whom shall I be sent to bear The Word —
That precious load — along the path to Heaven?

Almighty God! Eternal God! 'T is Thou,
That in Thy chosen servant here dost stand:
Prostrate before Thy footstool, lo, I bow,
To seek the dread commission at Thy hand.

O God, the Father! from whose quickening breath
All beings move, each in his proper round,
Whose arm sustains, above the abyss of Death,
What else would sink within that dread profound,

Give me, Great Parent, that enkindling power
To wake anew, deep in my brother's soul,

The Godlike nature, that, in man's first hour,
Made the dim part reflect the perfect whole.

O God, the Son! who, with unbounded grace,
Tookést up manhood, healedst the gaping wound,
And bearést to the Father's dwelling-place
The dying saved, the long-lost wanderer found,

Give unto me that ready neighbor-love,
That guideth where the wounded heart to find;
And give me Thy blest unction from above,
With holy balm the bleeding soul to bind.

O God, the Holy Ghost! that hallowest all
Thy faithful people, and to every truth
Upwards their still advancing steps dost call,
Till weary Age rests, smiling back on youth,

Hallow my life, that I may ever be
Worthy to stand at my King's festal board;
And teach me truth, that, being taught by Thee,
I may show others, where all good is stored.

One only God! whose works and ways are one,
Grant me with single heart to do Thy will,
Make me wrong thoughts and words and ways to
shun,
In Thy one, mystic realm my place to fill.

Keith Hall, Bermudas,
November 29, 1842, at night.

THE RELIEF OF LUCKNOW.

Are there not many that remember (who can can forget?) that scene in the Sikh war, — also in India, — when the distant gleam of arms and flash of friendly uniform was descried by a little exhausted army among the hills, and the Scotch pipes struck up "*Oh! but ye were lang a-comin!*" (Lachrymamne teneatis, amici? None of us, that have much Scottish blood, can keep our eyes from moistening.) The incident in the present case *may* not be historical, but it is true to nature, and intrinsically probable, which is all that poetry needs, in that respect.

OH! that last day in Lucknow fort!
We knew that it was the last;
That the enemy's mines had crept surely in,
And the end was coming fast.

To yield to that foe was worse than death;
And the men and we all worked on:
It was one day more, of smoke and roar,
And then it would all be done.

There was one of us, a Corporal's wife,
A fair, young, gentle thing,

Wasted with fever in the siege,
And her mind was wandering.

She lay on the ground, in her Scottish plaid,
And I took her head on my knee;
"When my father comes hame frae the pleugh," she said,
"Oh! please then waken me."

She slept like a child on her father's floor,
In the flecking of woodbine-shade,
When the house-dog sprawls by the half-open door,
And the mother's wheel is stayed.

It was smoke and roar and powder-stench,
And hopeless waiting for death;
But the soldier's wife, like a full-tired child,
Seemed scarce to draw her breath.

I sank to sleep, and I had my dream
Of an English village-lane,
And wall and garden; — but a wild scream
Brought me back to the roar again.

There Jessie Brown stood listening,
Until sudden gladness broke
All over her face, and she took my hand
And drew me near and spoke :

" *The Highlanders !* Oh ! dinna ye hear ?
The slogan far awa ?
The McGregor's ? Ah ! I ken it weel ;
It 's the grandest o' them a'.

" God bless thae bonny Highlanders !
We 're saved ! We 're saved ! " she cried ;
And fell on her knees, and thanks to God
Poured forth, like a full flood-tide.

Along the battery-line her cry
Had fallen among the men :
And they started ; for they were there to die ;
Was life so near them, then ?

They listened, for life ; and the rattling fire
Far off, and the far-off roar
Were all ; — and the Colonel shook his head,
And they turned to their guns once more.

Then Jessie said, "That slogan 's dune;
But can ye no hear them, noo,
'*The Campbells are comin'*? It 's no a dream;
Our succors hae broken through!"

We heard the roar and the rattle afar,
But the pipes we could not hear;
So the men plied their work of hopeless war,
And knew that the end was near.

It was not long ere it must be heard;
A shrilling, ceaseless sound;
It was no noise of the strife afar,
Or the sappers underground.

It *was* the pipes of the Highlanders,
And now they played "*Auld Lang Syne*,"
It came to our men, like the voice of God,
And they shouted along the line.

And they wept and shook one another's hands,
And the women sobbed in a crowd;
And every one knelt down where we stood,
And we all thanked God aloud.

That happy day, when we welcomed them,
Our men put Jessie first ;
And the General took her hand, and cheers
From the men, like a volley, burst.

And the pipers' ribbons and tartan streamed,
Marching round and round our line ;
And our joyful cheers were broken with tears,
For the pipes played "*Auld Lang Syne.*"

Saturday and Sunday nights,
January 2 and 3, 1858.

DIRGE TO A SOUL DEPARTING.

(FOR MUSIC.)

STAY, flitting soul!
Wilt thou not longer stay?
Why dost thou hasten on that weary way,
Beyond these quiet realms of day,
Into the unknown land, where dim mists roll?
Look back! Look back
Along the well-known track,
Stretching far backward to dear scenes of spring!
There childhood's pretty memories lie:
The flowing hair, the beamy eye,
The bounding step, and joyous, ringing cry.
See the glad hopes that erst
The child's true spirit nurst,
By day in visions bright,
In whispering dreams by night;
Dost thou not yearn towards them, as we sing?
And youth's first real strife
With the breasting waves of life,

When strength was in the arm,
And the heart was proud and warm,
And the eye looked forth, without alarm,
For all that time could bring.
See, see those sunny days!
And let our soft dirge raise
Bright tempting scenes before thine eye to fling!
Look! Look! This world is bright;
But now thou loved'st its light;
Why dost thou turn away thy sight,
As from an evil thing?
Come to us back! Come to us back!
Let not our sorrowing spirits lack
The fellowship to which our strong loves cling!

[*Weeping stillness.*]

Is it so hard for thee to linger yet
Where thou hast been at home these many years
Why should these long-familiar landings fret
Now, more then ever, that thou fain wilt set
This pleasant form aside, that we with tears
Must wash; then put away
Out of our sight forever and for aye?

Come to us back! Come to us back!
Come, yet a little, to our fond hearts back!

[*Stillness.*]

Why, why would'st thou forget
These once-loved voices, that, in every tone,
In days gone by, sweet influence have thrown
Around thee, answering warmly to thine own?
Wilt thou not listen? Hast thou no regret?
Wilt thou still forward, where is all unknown?
Wilt thou still forward?
And alone?
Oh! wilt thou venture such a path alone?
Turn! Turn! Come back! Come back!
Before thee how it gathers black!
Return, where all thou holdest dear are met!

[*Stillness.*]

Thou loiterest still;
We see these casements fill
With the soft-falling, gentle mist
Where thou art looking out, once more,
To see the scene long-known and loved before.

Hist! Hist!

This sternly-closéd door
From which glad words were wont to pour,
Is it forever closed? Will it not open more?
Is it in vain we list?
We mark, we mark its fixéd leaves
Tremble, as the soul yet heaves
Against them feebly, as in doubt
To open still to us that wait without;
Come, then! Oh, come!

[*Stillness.*]

But that faint, smothered cry!
Ah, smothered strife of agony!
Nay! we will let this weary body die!
Nay! flitting spirit, nay!
We will not have thee stay;
Go forward gladly on thy way;
Our songs shall cheer thee as thou goest home.

Farewell! Farewell! Close we these open eyes.
No more wilt thou be looking forth, this way,
Who once hast caught, afar, the light of Paradise.

Our love shall give this form to long decay,
That, when thou comest back for it, shall rise
A glorious body, at the Judgment-Day.

On! On! thou blessed soul! See Jesus wait;
Thy lamp of faith is trimmed, but all is light;
The path leads forward, to the open gate;
He waits thee smiling, and the way is bright.
On, faithful soul!
Our swelling songs shall roll
Sweet, melancholy surges here behind,
That full of memory thou shalt find
As one, slow-sailing from the outward shore
Of a dear land oft wandered o'er,
Hears, in still night, its wave-voice on the wind.
Thou art quitting, now, the verge
Of this long-belovéd land,
And mayest listen, still, the surge
Heave up upon the strand.
On! On! yet let our song
Still go with thee along,
Till it is lost amid the strain
Of Christ's glorious spirit-train

As another soul they gain
To sweet Paradise, no more to live, no more to love,
as here on earth, in vain.

Our earth-born dirges cease:
Pass, Christian soul, in peace!
Peace that Christ giveth:
PEACE!

January, 1846.

THE YEAR IS GONE!

WHERE art thou, O lost Year?
I tread upon the scattered leaves,
The way is drear; my lone heart grieves.
I see thy traces everywhere;
These leaves once decked thy golden hair.
I find thy playthings here;
But oh! thou art not near.

The bright and golden grain —
Men have it all long garnered in.
Here spreads the frosted stubble, thin,
O'er the wide fields whereon it stood,
Where thou didst trip, in playful mood,
Bringing the sun or rain.
I seek for thee in vain.

Is this thy merry brook,
Whose gurgling used to please thine ear?
Oh! my once happy, thoughtless Year!
Beneath its solid, icy roof,
How silent, now, it bides aloof!
Lost is the frolic look
That from thy smile it took.

Beneath the forest tall
No more I feel thy glowing breath,
Or watch the calm, too bright for death,
When thou at noon didst fall asleep,
And, what thy hands could no more keep,
Blossom or nut, would fall.
Sweet Year! In vain I call.

Thy pretty birds are mute,
That sang with all their little might
And flashed their bright wings in the light:
And children, fairer still than they,
Gambol no longer at their play:
No more the busy foot
Tramples the soft grass-root.

Thou wert no more the same
When once that hectic flush of red
Too surely on thy fair cheek spread;
And, by and by, in silent fold,
The white robes closed, all still and cold,
And when I called thy name,
No voice or answer came.

And there was deeper bond
Than such as various season weaves,
Of sunny flowers, or buds, or leaves:
I mourn for many a hope and thought
That by thy ministry were brought
Out of the world beyond:
These made my poor heart fond.

And I have wrought with thee,
In pleasant hours, at many a net,
Of hues, as when the sun doth set.
We stretched the strands out very wide,
But each too soon was thrust aside:
New schemes thou broughtest me
Of what could never be.

Thou knewest all I willed ;
How many purposes I made :
Into thine ear the whole was said,
How I would rue the ill deeds done,
How guilty temptings I would shun.
Now thy warm life is chilled,
What, of these plans, fulfilled !

O lost Year, be thou past !
Too soon the truant heart and will
All this clear sky of life would fill
With that unprofitable haze,
That makes half nights of working days.
Forward my way is cast ;
I rest not till the last.

1849.

BÜRGER'S LENORE.

LENORA rose at morning-red,
From bitter dreams awaking:
"Art faithless, William, or art dead,
So long thy love forsaking?"
He went with royal Frederic's might,
To battle in Prague's famous fight:
But from the war-field gory
No post has brought his story.

The King and Empress, tired, at last,
Of arms so vainly wielded,
Alike aside their rage have cast,
And to a truce have yielded.
Now each glad host with sing-song rang,
With beating drum and cling and clang;
And, decked with many a garland,
Came homeward from the far land.

And over all, all over all,
From street and lane and alley,
Shout old and young their jubel-call,
And round the home-march rally.
Praise God! the child and goodwife cried;
Welcome! said many a longing bride;
But, for Lenore, no meeting:
No kiss, or tender greeting.

Each way she flew, the ranks all through,
But, though all names were spoken,
No one that came her lover knew,
And no one could give token.
And when the hosts passed onward were,
She tore her glossy, raven hair;
Upon the greensward sinking,
With bitter woe past thinking.

The mother kneeled upon her knee;
"God, pity my poor daughter!
My darling child, what is 't with thee?"
And in her arms she caught her.
"Ah, mother, mother, gone is gone!

Now let the world and all be gone ! *
No pity dwells in Heaven :
Woe ! woe ! my heart is riven ! "

" Help, God ! oh, help ! look gently on !
Child, child ! oh, say, 'Our Father !'
What God does, that is sure well done :
God, judge not ; spare us rather ! "
" O mother, mother, mockery !
God has not, sure, well-done to me.
My prayers, ah ! what passed they for ?
Now nought is left to pray for ! "

" Help, God ! whoe'er the Father knows,
Knows He the children loveth ;
The Holy Sacrament such woes
As thine, my child, removeth."
" O mother, mother, little vent
My woe would find in sacrament.
No sacrament can solder
Forms that in death-damps moulder."

* Wherever a final word is repeated, the original has the same construction.

"Hear, child! How if the perjured one,
When long in far Hungáry,
Had all his ties of troth undone,
Some newer love to marry?
Cast off his heart, my child! by sin
In the long game he cannot win;
When soul and body sever,
This deed shall sting forever."

"O mother, mother, gone is gone!
Forsaken is forsaken,
Death, death! Come death, and I have won!
Why did I ever waken?
Go out, forever out, my light!
Die out, die out, in woe and night!
No pity dwells in Heaven;
Woe! woe! my soul is riven!"

"Help, God! To judgment enter not:
The poor child's heart is broken:
She utters, now, she knows not what:
Oh, count not what is spoken!

My child, forget this world's distress,
And think on God, and blessedness:
So to thy heart forsaken
A spouse shall yet be taken."

"O mother! What is blessedness?
Oh! what is hell, my mother?
With him, with him, is blessedness;
And hell without him, mother.
Go out, forever out, my light!
Die out, die out, in woe and night!
Without him, earth and heaven
In misery were even."

Thus mad despair within her brain,
And in her veins all revelled,
Till e'en at God's all-gracious reign,
Her impious scorn she levelled.
She wrung her hands and beat her breast
Until the sun went down to rest:
Till up to heaven's high chamber
The golden stars 'gan clamber.

And then without, hark! tramp, tramp, tramp!
A horse's footsteps sounded;
Then on the steps, with heavy stamp,
The clanking rider bounded.
And hark! and hark! the door-bell ring,
All gently, softly, ching-ling-ling.
Then, through the door-leaves uttered,
Just these quick questions fluttered:

"Holla! holla! undo, my child!
Wak'st thou, my love, or sleepest?
Has time thy love for me beguiled?
And smilest thou, or weepest?"
"Ah, William! Thou, so late at night?
I've wept and waked, in weary plight;
Oh! bitter woe I've tasted.
Whence hast thou hither hasted?"

"Near midnight 't is, we saddle steed;
From Boehmen I rode hither:
Ere I could mount, 't was late indeed,
And we go back together."

"O William, first a moment stay:
The blast roars through the hawthorn spray:
Come to my arms, heart-dearest!
Here no cold wind thou fearest."

"Through hawthorn spray let fierce blasts roar,
And ravage, helter-skelter!
The wild steed paws, and clinks the spur;
I dare not here seek shelter.
Come, dress thee: spring and swing, with speed,
Behind me, here, upon my steed.
A hundred miles I take thee,
This day my bride to make thee."

"Alas! a hundred miles would'st thou
Bear me, *this day*, to bridal?
Hark, hark! the clock is clanging now;
Eleven struck: 'T is idle!"
"Look far; look near; the moon shines clear
We and the dead ride fast, my dear;
I gage, ere night 's at highest,
Thou in thy bride-bed liest."

"Say on, where is thy chamber, dear?
What bride-bed dost thou tender?"
"Still, cool and small; far, far from here;
Six wide boards and two slender."
"Hast room for me?" "For thee and me:
Come, dress thee: mount; I stay for thee.
The marriage-guests have waited:
We must not be belated."

Fairly she dressed her, sprang and swung
Herself to horse behind him;
Fast to the well-loved rider clung,
And with white arms entwined him.
Then hurtling off, with leap and bound,
At whistling speed they scoured the ground,
Till horse and rider panted,
And sparks and dust far slanted.

On this and on the other hand,
How flew the plains and ridges;
Hillock and rock and meadow-land;
How thundered all the bridges!

"My love, dost fear? The moon shines clear:
Hurrah! The dead ride fast, my dear!
My love, dost fear the dead men?"
"Ah, no! yet leave the dead men!'

What clang and song swept there along,
Where the foul ravens flaunted?
Hark! death-bell clang! Hark! funeral-song!
"Bear on the dead!" is chanted.
And nearer drew a funeral-train:
Coffin and bier came on, amain:
Their song the dark quire pitches
Like the frogs' cry in ditches.

"Nay, bury after midnight-tide,
With clang and song and weeping:
I bear me home my fair young bride:
Come to our merry-keeping.
Come clerk! come here! your quire all bring,
Come all, the bridal-song to sing,
Come, priest, the blessing say us
Ere we in bride-bed lay us."

Ceased clang and song ; the bier was gone :
They came as they were bidden,
And, hurry-skurry, trampled on
Fast as the steed was ridden.
And ever on, with leap and bound,
At whistling speed they scoured the ground ;
Both horse and rider panted,
And sparks and dust far slanted.

How flew, on right, how flew, on left,
Hills, trees, and hedgéd spaces !
How flew, on left and right and left,
Towns, cities, dwelling-places !
" My love, dost fear ? The moon shines clear :
Hurrah ! The dead ride well, my dear ;
My love, dost fear the dead men ? "
" Ah ! let them rest, the dead men ! "

See there ! see there ! On gallows-height,
Dance round the wheel's curst swivel,
Half-seen within the moon's pale light,
Spectres, in airy revel.

"Sasa! ye spectres. Here! come here!
Come, spectres, come, and follow near,
Our wedding reels to number
Ere we lie down to slumber."

And lo! the spectres, rush, rush, rush!
Behind the wild train hurtle,
As whirls the storm-wind's sudden gush
Through withered leaves of myrtle.
And on and on, with leap and bound,
At whistling speed they scoured the ground;
Both horse and rider panted,
And sparks and dust far slanted.

How flew the scenes in moonlight spread!
How into farness flitted!
And how, their places overhead,
The sky and planets quitted!
"My love, dost fear? The moon shines clear;
Hurrah! The dead ride well, my dear;
My love, dost fear the dead men?"
"Ah, woe! Let rest the dead men!"

"Steed, steed! methinks the cock crows there;
Soon will the sands be wasted;
Steed, steed! I scent the morning air;
Haste, as thou hast not hasted!
'T is o'er, 't is o'er! Our course is o'er!
The chamber stands with open door;
The dead ride wondrous races;
Here, here, we find our places."

Against an iron churchyard door,
The furious courser battered:
Its clamps fell loose, the shock before,
And post and bar were shattered.
Its clanking leaves wide open flew,
And o'er the graves the train swept through.
Gravestones were seen to glimmer
Round in the moon's pale shimmer.

See, see! An instant scarce can flit,
Ere, hoo! a fearful wonder!
The rider's flesh, all bit by bit,
Like cinders fell asunder.

Like kernel bare, without the hull,
His head became a naked skull;
His body shrunk and narrow,
With hour-glass and with arrow.

Snorted the steed, and madly reared;
Fierce fiery flashes spurted;
Then hey! sank down and disappeared,
And she lay there deserted.
A howl, a howl from out the lift!
A yell from forth each grave's deep rift!
Lenora's spirit shivers:
'Twixt death and life it quivers.

Now featly danced, in moonlight-glance,
All round about in mazes,
The spectre-forms a fetter-dance,
And howled in such-like phrases;
"Be meek, though heart should break in twain,
Nor dare thy God in heaven arraign.
Thy dust to this still city!
God show thy soul his pity!"

June, 1846.

THE BARREN FIELD.

Here I labor, weak and lone,
Ever, ever sowing seed;
Ever tending what is sown:
Little is my gain, indeed.

Weary day and restless night
Follow in an endless round;
Wastes my little human might:
Soon my place will not be found.

Why so stubborn is my field?
Why does little fruit appear?
What an hundred-fold should yield,
Now goes barren all the year.

Rank weeds crowd and jostle there,
Nodding vainly in the sun:

But the plants, for which I care,
I may till them, one by one.

After all the sun and rain,
Weak and yellow drooping things,
From the lean earth, turned in vain,
These are all my labor wrings!

Oh, my Lord, the field is Thine:
Why do I, with empty pride,
Call the little garden mine,
When my work is Thine, beside?

If I claim it for my own,
Thou wilt give me its poor gain;
And, at harvest, I, alone,
May bring fruits to Thee in vain.

If I give myself to Thee
For Thy work, all poor and mean,
As Thou pleasest it shall be,
If I much or little glean:

Yet Thou wilt not spurn my toil,
Or my offering, at the last,
If, from off this meagre soil,
At Thy feet my all is cast.

Other work for man is none,
But to do the Master's will ;
Wet with rain, or parched with sun,
Meekly I Thy garden till.

April 28, 1849.

CHRIST'S LEGACY.

Who deems that Holy Church has lost
  The priceless gift the Saviour gave?
Or, as an idle bauble, tost
  Beneath the curst world's hungry wave,
Her keys that, all this wide world o'er,
Oped to man's want God's spirit-store?
That now the Kingdom is but earth alone
Where man's poor sight and wisdom seek their own?

Who deems that hidden Paradise, —
  Its sweet cool shades, its living streams,
Its lustrous air, from seraphs' eyes
  Radiant with interwoven beams,
And the eternal Light divine
Filling up all with changeless shine, —
That these, and converse with the dwellers there,
To men in spirit are not free as air?

That His blest kingdom, — which, Christ said,
  Should ever stand while earth doth stand ;
And, when the last flames, fierce and red,
  Should melt and burn up sea and land,
Transfigured through those fires should glow
Thenceforth no earthliness to know, —
That this hath not one, only, changeless frame,
One as the Lord : on earth, in heaven, the same ?

Or that the Body of the Lord,
  The Godhead dwelling in the flesh, —
Is not, to us, as when that Word
  In human nature dwelt afresh ?
Or that God's fulness, now, as then,
Doth not inhabit in us men,
A fulness that in each of us hath place
Of grace according to our growth in grace ?

Oh ! is not God the selfsame now
  As when he put on human frame ?
His Body is the Church : and how
  Is this, his Body, not the same ?

It is the same where'er Faith is :
Christ manifests himself in His :
Where Faith is not, to them is Christ no more
Indwelling, in the Spirit, as of yore.

This glorious kingdom — rich within,
  And glowing with all spirit-powers —
There is no cause, but each man's sin,
  If all its treasures be not ours :
Our priests are gifted with the Word,
And every member of the Lord
Hath his own measure of the Holy Ghost :
In the most humble and obedient, most.

And in the Spirit, oh, what height
  The feet of faithful men do mount !
There glossy slopes flow all with light,
  And vales are rich with stream and fount.
The pure see God on every side ;
Them spirits gently serve and guide,
While earth, to them, is sorrow, shame, and ill,
The church is heaven on earth, about them still.

Sweet mysteries to them that love,
  Do lead to that eye hath not seen;
An open sky is spread above
  Wherein no cloud hath ever been.
The Word wells full in every heart;
Deep calleth unto deep, apart;
And Love, God's being, maketh them all one
In Him, the Father, who are in the Son.

1849.

A BURIAL-HYMN.

TO BE SUNG ON THE WAY TO THE GRAVE.

We bring Thee, Lord, this little dust
  To lay in earth away :
In thy sure watch we meekly trust
  To keep it for the Day.

Thy will be done ! This dust, all dead,
  Must lose its fairer form,
And graces in the deep grave shed
  That almost yet are warm.

We thank Thee for the little while
  Our child lived here in love,
To glad a narrow place with smiles
  As from Thy house above.

And more, oh ! we must thank Thee more
  That dew of upper day
Baptized his earthly being o'er,
  And spirit hallowed clay.

TO GOD, MOST HIGH.

O MY Lord, I have but Thee;
Other friends are faint and few,
To myself I am not true;
Yet, my God, Thou lovest me.

I am poor and have no more
But Thy love within my heart;
Earth shall never tear apart
That which is my hidden store.

Many, many doubts and fears,
I have many pains and cares;
But Thou comest, at unawares,
And I see Thee through my tears.

I would never be my own,
Nor on friends my heart-strings twine;
I do seek to be but Thine,
And to love but Thee alone.

Jesus! while Thy cross I see,
Though my heart do bleed with woe,
By those blessed streams I know,
Blood of Thine was shed for me.

O my Lord! Be Thou my guide;
Let me hold Thee by the hand,
Then, in drear and barren land,
I will seek no friend beside.

January 7, 1848.

LOVE DISPOSED OF.

HERE goes Love! Now cut him clear,
A weight about his neck:
If he linger longer here,
Our ship will be a wreck.
Overboard! Overboard!
Down let him go!
In the deep he may sleep,
Where the corals grow.

He said he'd woo the gentle breeze,
A bright tear in her eye;
But she was false or hard to please,
Or he has told a lie.
Overboard! Overboard!
Down in the sea
He may find a truer mind,
Where the mermaids be.

He sang us many a merry song
While the breeze was kind :
But he has been lamenting long
The falseness of the wind.
Overboard ! Overboard !
Under the wave
Let him sing where smooth shells ring
In the ocean's cave.

He may struggle ; he may weep ;
We'll be stern and cold ;
His grief will find, within the deep,
More tears than can be told.
He has gone overboard !
We will float on ;
We shall find a truer wind
Now that he is gone.

1839.

TO MY OLD PARISHIONERS,

ON WRITING A TALE OF NEWFOUNDLAND.

THE parish-priest that hath his charge,
Beside the stormy sea,
Where howling tempests stalk at large,
And many an iceberg, as a barge,
Moors where the shallows be ;
Where winter's sky, with sudden gust,
Is traversed to and fro,
And storm-clouds, broken up as dust,
Fill earth all deep with snow,
Hath much to speak of hardy men
That face the wild sea-gale,
And loving hearts made dreary, when
The waiting eyes must fail,
That from the cliffs their far search strain
To see, slow-toiling home again,
The long-familiar sail
That shall not come ; for it is tost
Like drifting weed above the lost,

Who down and down, through soundless deep,
Have found a pathway, sheer and steep,
And at the foot shall lie and sleep,
While long the hamlet's tale
Lingers upon their unknown fate,
And, night by night, the fire burns late
In one sad, silent cot,
Where wife and children spread their hands
And cower above the wasting brands,
And the poor house-dog understands,
Why they that went come not.

Often when holy prayers are said
Beside a new-made grave,
Some mother waileth for *her* dead;
She never held his heavy head
And mother's tears upon it shed
Ere dust to dust she gave.
He lieth where no foot may tread,
No little ones may there be led,
Where long, lank ocean-weeds are spread,
Beneath the shifting wave.

Sometimes, before accustomed date,
A boat comes lonely back, —
No colors flaunt, in joyful state,
Above her silent track :
She bringeth not accustomed freight,
But laboreth with some strange weight :
The air is chill and desolate
That breathes around her way
As from the iceberg, cold and lone,
A stern, far-reaching chill is thrown
Abroad upon the day.
The skipper, from the helm, looks on
With fixèd eye and visage wan,
And hath no word to say.
The neighbors, gathered on the beach,
Gaze wistfully ; and, each to each,
Breaking long pauses in their speech,
Conjecture, as they may.
Some one has dreamed, within the night,
" The minister, in clothing white,
Beside a grave did stand,
With head all bare, as reading prayer,
He held his book in hand.

Dark mourners, bending low around,
Wetted with silent tears the ground
And the rough grave-pit scanned.
Over-against them, on the east,
Were angel-forms, whereof the least
Was glorious and grand.
And, at the words, one scattered dust,
With bright hand on the coffin's crust,
And forth a form as of the Just,
Went with them to their land."
The simple men, that hear this dream,
Ask reverent questions, for they deem
Such things, how strange soe'er they seem,
No matter for a smile.
Now say they, as the boat sweeps by,
"The skipper's eldest son doth lie
Coffined within her, for his eye
Looked spirit-like, erewhile."
Ay, ay! And it is even so!
Soon flits about the news of woe:
"When the Lord's day comes round,
The long procession, sad and slow,
Mounting the churchyard hill shall go,

To lay the young man's body low,
In consecrated ground."

Such are full-frequent things with those
That dwell beside the sea:
Whose sails feel every wind that blows,
If fair or foul it be.
Dear patient fisherman! for you
Whom late I lived among,
My heart, that loved you, yearns anew,
And often pass before my view
The forms of old and young.
For love of you this tale I tell
Of things now long agone;
And as the dark and heavy swell
Of memory heaves on,
With wrecks of loves once builded well
As if to live for aye,
Ye may shed tears like those which fell
From him that wrote this lay
And who again now says farewell!
As he will always pray.

February, 1848.

THE TEMPTER AT THE SIDE.

SEEST thou the shadow dogging at thy feet,
Without the breath of any at thy side?
Lo! there is one whom thou shalt never meet
Though thou do travel earth, both long and wide;
Never in lonely field, — in crowded street, —
In joy or grief: whatever thee betide,
To meet thee face to face, nowhere shall he abide.
Seest thou it at thy feet?
Know'st thou him at thy side?

He has been nigh thee since thy tottering pace
First faltered, doubtful, from thy mother's hand;
Anigh thee, yet, he hath his constant place,
Now that with strong men thou hast taken stand.
Go as thou wilt, thou winnest not the race;
Stay where thou wilt, in this or farthest land,
Untired he leaves thee not, whose face thou hast not
scanned.

He ever hath his place :
Ever is he at hand.

Albeit in the growing time of night
When the green things are starting everywhere,
And bud and leaf, sure of its tiny right,
Stretches towards its God for its blest share,
Then on thy longing mind celestial might
Has lighted down, and with quick vigor there
Has settled deep and still, — yet, not the less, beware!
Not present to thy sight,
The dark one loitered there.

Albeit in the stir and throng of men,
Catching warm influence from the glance of eye,
And thrill of words, that full and fragrant, then,
Go kindling to the heart, ere they will die,
Thou hast not slumbered, — nor been coward, when,
If need were, thy lone voice must rise on high,
And thou go lone through all, — yet then that One
was nigh,
Amid the crowd of men
On thee he kept his eye.

Albeit in the home's dear sunny scene,
Where low and homelike sounds, of birds and bees,
Float ever, streaming through that sea of sheen
And wide peace bounds the world's strange haunts
from thee :
In that, — man's noblest place, — thy soul has been
Like a blest soul, familiar and at ease,
Sharing a heavenly love that sin could never seize,
He was in that pure scene,
Though thou wast all at ease.

Bethink thee how thy well-kept heart has known
Quick-starting thoughts, a frightful, poisonous growth;
Bethink thee how suggestions not thine own
Have crept and overcome it, slow and loth ;
How a foul breath, o'er its bright vision blown,
Has buried all in the thick fog of sloth :
Dost thou not know him, yet, tempter and sharer,
both ?
He all thy moods has known,
When willing and when loth.

God set that shadow dogging at thy feet,
To warn thee one was ever at thy side

Whate'er thy state, to pour in promptings meet
From heavenly-guided life to draw thee wide.
Therefore by day that shade doth near thee fleet,
Nor in the night that shadow is denied
When for God's light of day man's light has been
supplied :
Dark shadow at thy feet,
Dark foe is at thy side.

November 3 and 4, 1847.

A RHYME READ BY TWO LOVERS.

THE earth, without, was dark and very still :
No loving moon leaned downwards from the night
To draw forth, out of darkness, vale and hill,
And wooded town, and far stream glistening white ;
And with her patient, maiden-modest skill,
Set the whole silent scene before her sight ;
And the near park
Was still and dark,
And night and stillness, more than all
Clung to the trees beside the wet house-wall.
No insect's hum, nor bat-wing's whirring stroke,
Nor sudden cry the night's thick stillness broke.

Cool through the casement came light evening airs
From off the meadows wet with summer-rain :
At times a rain-drop, shaken unawares,
Dripped from its hold, held long but held in vain.
The gauzy curtain, flowered, slight and frail,
Swelled with the soft air, like a pleasure-sail ;

And, in the room, a rich, soft radiance fell
From the high, shaded lamp, on graceful things
Which woman knows to choose and set so well
That from her mere warm touch a new grace clings;
And now, in that most still of summer eves,
Within the circle of the lamp's mild glow,
A youth and maiden turned the pictured leaves
Of a fair book ; their two heads bending so
That each hears how the other's young heart heaves:
(Ah ! think we of our own loves, long ago ?)
Her wreathéd, glossy hair now brushed his cheek ;
Now their quick eyes, by one sure, common thrill,
Rose toward each other's, and they did not speak,
For strongest, quick-winged speech
Has never learned to reach
Where love's fair meaning looks from cloudless height.
Then she first dropped her slow lids, strong and meek,
And both turned to their task, as with one will ;
For two like these, knowing that subtile might
Fills all their features to the utmost grace,
Fear to show this beside each other's sight ;

Scarce themselves dare to read other's face ;
For their deep lives have surely mined, below,
Each toward the other, through the wall between,
Which soon shall fall, at some slight, sudden blow,
And one wide love be where two hearts have been.
O dear young love ! Young love most bright !
Thou fairest thing this earth can show !
Old eyes will moisten at the sight,
Old hearts will feel the once-known glow !

A comely lady sat apart ;
It might be she was deep in thought ;
It might be that her very heart
Must go with what her fingers wrought ;
Never by any chance
Her calm, wise matron-glance
That happy scene of young love sought.

A child, as fresh as that night's breeze,
Bright as the gone day's light,
Holding her own book on her knees,
Beneath her fast-fixed sight,
With many a half-frayed golden curl,

Sat near the lover's seat:
Through sudden leap and race and whirl,
Chasing some story fleet,
Or asking oft, with knitted brow,
The little-heeding lovers, how
The words and sense could meet.
Her little unripe heart recks less
Of their delicious silentness.

The maiden's father, too, whate'er
His stately thoughts or fancies were,
Seemed, by all senses save of sight,
(Unlike the mother, calm and wise,)
Drawn to that circle of the light
Where the two felt each other's eyes.
And so, in that most still of summer-eves,
The youth and maiden turned their pictured leaves.

"Read to me here," she said, and laid her hand,
Her soft, warm hand, on his, to point him where:
"Of 'The Night's Guest,' that I may understand
Why there is pictured here a churchyard bare
With rounded graves and tombs within the wall

And the tall, shadowing yew-trees over all.
Why Death stands here, within this open door,
That the old man waits, wearily, before."
The youth glanced at the picture while she said
Her gentle words, — and longer, — and then read:

THE NIGHT'S GUEST.

In the evening, cold and dreary,
  Knocketh one at hostel-door,
All the way looks dark before
  As the way behind was weary.

"Host! Hast thou a chamber quiet?
  I have come a weary way:
Fain would rest till early day,
  Far from wicked din of riot."

"I have many a quiet chamber,
  Out of reach of human call:
And upon the outer wall
  Scented briar and cypress clamber."

" Quick ! O Friend ! I may not tarry,
  I am all with toil forespent :
And my aching knees are bent
  With the weary weight I carry."

Rough voiced was the Host and surly,
  Yet he spake in softened tone :
" Hast a load, and art alone ?
  Go not to thy rest so early."

" Host, I am with travel broken :
  Slumber weigheth on my eyes :
Yet I take in courteous wise
  What in courteous wise was spoken.

" Lo ! the load, that doth me cumber,
  'T is but this my body's weight;
I have borne it far and late ;
  Now I long for restful slumber."

" Yet I give but friendly warning,"
  Said the Host in softened tone ;
" Why, then, wilt thou go alone,
  Since thou goest at early morning ? "

"Host! I go not hence unfriended,
  I have comrades for the way.
Now no longer bid me stay;
  Let this longsome day be ended."

"Yea! but I have chambers many,
  Meet for many a different guest;
One in hallowed bed hath rest,
  One lies down unblest of any."

"Not so far I come unshriven;
  Weeping sore I sought release:
To my soul was spoken peace;
  Pledges twain to me were given."

"Yet forgive me: though thou seekest,
  Weary, nought but welcome rest,
Take my warning, O my Guest,
  Prove those things whereof thou speakest.

"Art thou of the Holy number?
  Dost thou know the Blessed Lord?
Canst thou give the Holy Word?
  Thou in hallowed bed shalt slumber."

"I may claim by Holy Mother,
For the Blood that stained the Tree;
And the Word she gave to me
Is, The Cross: I know no other."

"Now no more I may deny thee;
Chide me not, mine honored guest,
That I kept thee from thy rest;
'T was the King that bade me try thee.

"Waiteth now thy quiet chamber,
Thou wilt lie in hallowed bed,
Cross's sign above thy head,
O'er the wall shall roses clamber."

"Thou hast well those pledges taken —
Be thy slumber calm and sweet,
Till at early day, thou greet
Him whose voice shall thee awaken."

So with courteous word and gesture
Went the host before his guest:
Lighted him to place of rest:
Help'd him doff his soiléd vesture.

Laid him down in chamber quiet,
He that came from weary way,
Resting until early day,
Far from wicked din of riot.

The two were graver when the tale was done :
Then said the maiden, gently, " But one thing,
One human thing, shall last ; oh, surely one ! "
And he said " Yes ! no changing time can bring
A change to this ! " So said he for her ear ;
And when they parted, wishing, each, " Good night ! "
Again she said, " Life's journey is not drear :
I see a pathway long and very bright."
So said she, with her voice most kind and dear,
And their two loves met at each other's lip.
Can life be drear that has such fellowship ?
" If it be God's — " she said, and she was right :
Peace to thee, O dear love ! Good night ! Good night !
For not till youth, and life, and death, is o'er,
Shall this life's love, made heavenly, be no more.
And the short story of the tired Night's Guest
Shows how that love at even goes to rest.

1847, 1859.

THE BRAVE OLD SHIP, THE ORIENT.

Woe for the brave ship Orient!
Woe for the old ship Orient!
For in broad, broad light, and with land in sight,
Where the waters bubbled white,
One great sharp shriek! One shudder of affright! —
And —
down went the brave old ship, the Orient!

It was the fairest day in the merry month of May,
And sleepiness had settled on the seas;
And we had our white sail set, high up, and higher yet,
And our flag flashed and fluttered at its ease;
The Cross of St. George, that in mountain and in gorge, —
On the hot and dusty plain, —
On the tiresome, trackless main, —
Conquering out, — conquering home again, —
Had flamed, the world over, on the breeze.

Ours was the far-famed Albion,
And she had her best look of might and beauty
on,
As she swept across the seas that day.
The wind was fair and soft, both alow and aloft
And we wore the even hours away.

The steadying sun heaved up, as day drew on,
And there grew a long swell of the sea.
And, first in upper air, then under, everywhere,
From the topmost towering sail
Down, down to quarter-rail,
The wind began to breathe more free.
It was soon to breathe its last,
For a wild and bitter blast
Was the master of that stormy day to be.

"Ho! Hilloa! A sail!" was the topman's hail:
"A sail, hull-down upon our lee!"
Then with sea-glass to his eye,
And his gray locks blowing by,
The Admiral sought what she might be.
And from top, and from deck,

Was it ship? Was it wreck? A far-off, far-off
speck,
Of a sudden we found upon our lee.

On the round waters wide, floated no thing beside,
But we and the stranger sail:
And a hazy sky, that threatened storm,
Came coating the heaven so blue and warm,
And ahead hung the portent of a gale;
A black bank hanging there
When the order came, to wear,
Was remembered, ever after, in the tale.

Across the long, slow swell
That scarcely rose and fell,
The wind began to blow out of the cloud;
And scarce an hour was gone ere the gale was
fairly on,
And through our strained rigging howled aloud.
Before the stormy wind, that was maddening behind,
We gathered in our canvas farthest spread.
Black clouds had started out
From the heavens all about,

And the welkin grew all black overhead.
But though stronger and more strong
The fierce gale rushed along,
The stranger brought her old wind in her breast.
Up came the ship from the far-off sea,
And on with the strong wind's breath rushed we.
She grew to the eye, against the clouded sky,
And eagerly her points and gear we guessed.
As we made her out, at last,
She was maimed in spar and mast
And she hugged the easy breeze for rest.

We could see the old wind fail
At the nearing of our gale;
We could see them lay their course with the wind:
Still we neared and neared her fast,
Hurled on by our fierce blast,
With the seas tumbling headlong behind.
She had come out of some storm, and, in many
a busy swarm,
Her crew were refitting, as they might,
The wreck of upper spars
That had left their ugly scars,

As if the ship had come out of a fight.
We scanned her well, as we drifted by:
A strange old ship, with her poop built high,
And with quarter-galleries wide,
And a huge beaked prow, as no ships are builded
now,
And carvings all strange, beside.
A Byzantine bark, and a ship of name and mark
Long years and generations ago;
Ere any mast or yard of ours was growing hard
With the seasoning of long Norwegian snow.
She was the brave old Orient,
The old imperial Orient,
Brought down from times afar
Not such as our ships are,
But unchanged in hull and unchanged in spar,
Since mighty ships of war were builded so.

Down her old black side poured the water in a tide,
As they toiled to get the better of a leak:
We had got a signal set in the shrouds,
And our men through the storm looked on in
crowds: —

But for wind, we were near enough to speak.
It seemed her sea and sky were in times long,
long gone by,
That we read in winter-evens about;
As if to other stars
She had reared her old-world spars,
And her hull had kept an old-time ocean out.
We saw no signal fly, and her men scarce lifted
eye,
But toiled at the work that was to do;
It warmed our English blood
When across the stormy flood,
We saw the old ship and her crew.
The glories and the memories of other days agone
Seemed clinging to the old ship, as in storm she
labored on.
The old ship Orient!
The brave, imperial Orient!

All that stormy night through, our ship was lying-to
Whenever we could keep her to the wind;
But late in the next day we gained a quiet bay,
For the tempest had left us far behind.

So before the sunny town
Went our anchors splashing down ;
Our sails we hung all out to the sun ;
While airs from off the steep
Came playing at bo-peep
With our canvas, hour by hour, in their fun.
We leaned on boom or rail with many a lazy tale
Of the work of the storm that had died ;
And watched, with idle eyes,
Our floats, like summer flies,
Riding lazily about the ship's side.
Suddenly they cried, from the other deck,
That the Orient was gone to wreck !
That her hull lay high on a broken shore,
And the brave old ship would float no more.
But we heard a sadder tale, ere the night came on,
And a truer tale, of the ship that was gone.
They had seen from the height,
As she came from yester-night,
While the storm had not gone by, and the sea was
running high,
A ship driving heavily to land ;
A strange great ship, (so she seemed to be

While she tumbled and rolled on the far-off sea,
And strange when she toiled, near at hand,)
But some ship of mark and fame,
Though crippled, then, and lame,
And that must have been gallantly manned.
So she came, driving fast ;
They could tell her men, at last ;
There were harbors down the coast on her lee ;
When, strangely, she broached to, —
Then, with her gallant crew,
Went headlong down into the sea.

That was the Orient ;
The brave old Orient :
Such a ship as never more will be.

1857 and 1860.

☞ Any Books in this list will be sent free of postage, on receipt of price.

Boston, 135 Washington Street,
March, 1860.

A LIST OF BOOKS

PUBLISHED BY

TICKNOR AND FIELDS.

Sir Walter Scott.

Illustrated Household Edition of the Waverley Novels. In portable size, 16mo. form. Now Complete. Price 75 cents a volume.

The paper is of fine quality; the stereotype plates are not old ones repaired, the type having been cast expressly for this edition. The Novels are illustrated with capital steel plates engraved in the best manner, after drawings and paintings by the most eminent artists, among whom are Birket Foster, Darley, Billings, Landseer, Harvey, and Faed. This Edition contains all the latest notes and corrections of the author, a Glossary and Index; and some curious additions, especially in "Guy Mannering" and the "Bride of Lammermoor;" being the fullest edition of the Novels ever published. *The notes are at the foot of the page*,—a great convenience to the reader.

Any of the following Novels sold separate.

Waverley, 2 vols.
Guy Mannering, 2 vols.
The Antiquary, 2 vols.
Rob Roy, 2 vols.
Old Mortality, 2 vols.
Black Dwarf, Legend of Montrose, } 2 vols.
Heart of Mid Lothian, 2 vols.
Bride of Lammermoor, 2 vols.
Ivanhoe, 2 vols.
The Monastery, 2 vols.
The Abbot, 2 vols.
Kenilworth, 2 vols.
The Pirate, 2 vols.
The Fortunes of Nigel, 2 vols.
Peveril of the Peak, 2 vols.
Quentin Durward, 2 vols.
St. Ronan's Well, 2 vols.
Redgauntlet, 2 vols.
The Betrothed, The Highland Widow, } 2 vols.
The Talisman, Two Drovers, My Aunt Margaret's Mirror, The Tapestried Chamber, The Laird's Jock. } 2 vols.
Woodstock, 2 vols.
The Fair Maid of Perth, 2 vols.
Anne of Geierstein, 2 vols.
Count Robert of Paris, 2 vols.
The Surgeon's Daughter, Castle Dangerous, Index and Glossary. } 2 vols.

Thomas De Quincey.

Confessions of an English Opium-Eater, and Suspiria de Profundis. With Portrait. 75 cents.

Biographical Essays. 75 cents.

Miscellaneous Essays. 75 cents.

The Cæsars. 75 cents.

Literary Reminiscences. 2 vols. $1.50.

Narrative and Miscellaneous Papers. 2 vols. $1.50.

Essays on the Poets, &c. 1 vol. 16mo. 75 cents.

Historical and Critical Essays. 2 vols. $1.50.

Autobiographic Sketches. 1 vol. 75 cents.

Essays on Philosophical Writers, &c. 2 vols. 16mo. $1.50.

Letters to a Young Man, and other Papers. 1 vol. 75 cents.

Theological Essays and other Papers. 2 vols. $1.50.

The Note Book. 1 vol. 75 cents.

Memorials and other Papers. 2 vols. 16mo. $1.50.

The Avenger and other Papers. 1 vol. 75 cents.

Logic of Political Economy, and other Papers. 1 vol. 75 cents.

Alfred Tennyson.

Poetical Works. With Portrait. 2 vols. Cloth. $2.00.

Pocket Edition of Poems Complete. 75 cents.

The Princess. Cloth. 50 cents.

In Memoriam. Cloth. 75 cents.

Maud, and other Poems. Cloth. 50 cents.

Idyls of the King. A new volume. Cloth. 75 cents.

Barry Cornwall.

English Songs and other Small Poems. $1.00.

Dramatic Poems. Just published. $1.00.

Essays and Tales in Prose. 2 vols. $1.50.

Henry W. Longfellow.

POETICAL WORKS. In two volumes. 16mo. Boards. $2.00.

POCKET EDITION OF POETICAL WORKS. In two volumes. $1.75.

POCKET EDITION OF PROSE WORKS COMPLETE. In two volumes. $1.75.

THE SONG OF HIAWATHA. $1.00.

EVANGELINE: A TALE OF ACADIE. 75 cents.

THE GOLDEN LEGEND. A POEM. $1.00.

HYPERION. A ROMANCE. $1.00.

OUTRE-MER. A PILGRIMAGE. $1.00.

KAVANAGH. A TALE. 75 cents.

THE COURTSHIP OF MILES STANDISH. 1 vol. 16mo. 75 cents.

Illustrated editions of EVANGELINE, POEMS, HYPERION, THE GOLDEN LEGEND, and MILES STANDISH.

Charles Reade.

PEG WOFFINGTON. A NOVEL. 75 cents.

CHRISTIE JOHNSTONE. A NOVEL. 75 cents.

CLOUDS AND SUNSHINE. A NOVEL. 75 cents.

'NEVER TOO LATE TO MEND.' 2 vols. $1.50.

WHITE LIES. A NOVEL. 1 vol. $1.25.

PROPRIA QUÆ MARIBUS and THE BOX TUNNEL. 25 cts.

William Howitt.

LAND, LABOR, AND GOLD. 2 vols. $2.00.

A BOY'S ADVENTURES IN AUSTRALIA. 75 cents.

James Russell Lowell.

COMPLETE POETICAL WORKS. In Blue and Gold. 2 vols. $1.50.

POETICAL WORKS. 2 vols. 16mo. Cloth. $1.50.

SIR LAUNFAL. New Edition. 25 cents.

A FABLE FOR CRITICS. New Edition. 50 cents.

THE BIGLOW PAPERS. A New Edition. 63 cents.

Nathaniel Hawthorne.

Twice-Told Tales. Two volumes. $1.50.
The Scarlet Letter. 75 cents.
The House of the Seven Gables. $1.00.
The Snow Image, and other Tales. 75 cents.
The Blithedale Romance. 75 cents.
Mosses from an Old Manse. 2 vols. $1.50.
Transformation; or, The Romance of Monte Beni. 2 vols. $1.50.
True Stories from History and Biography. With four fine Engravings. 75 cents.
A Wonder-Book for Girls and Boys. With seven fine Engravings. 75 cents.
Tanglewood Tales. Another "Wonder-Book." With Engravings. 88 cents.

Charles Kingsley.

Two Years Ago. A New Novel. $1.25.
Amyas Leigh. A Novel. $1.25.
Glaucus; or, the Wonders of the Shore. 50 cts.
Poetical Works. 75 cents.
The Heroes; or, Greek Fairy Tales. 75 cents.
Andromeda and other Poems. 50 cents.
Sir Walter Raleigh and his Time, &c. $1.25.
New Miscellanies. 1 vol. $1.00.

Coventry Patmore.

The Angel in the House. Betrothal.
" " " " Espousals. 75 cts. each.

George S. Hillard.

Six Months in Italy. 1 vol. 16mo. $1.50.
Dangers and Duties of the Mercantile Profession. 25 cents.
Selections from the Writings of Walter Savage Landor. 1 vol. 16mo. 75 cents.

Oliver Wendell Holmes.

POEMS. With fine Portrait. Boards. $1.00. Cloth. $1.12.

ASTRÆA. Fancy paper. 25 cents.

THE AUTOCRAT OF THE BREAKFAST TABLE. With Illustrations by Hoppin. 16mo. $1.00.

The Same. Large Paper Edition. 8vo. Tinted paper. $3.00.

THE PROFESSOR AT THE BREAKFAST TABLE. 16mo. $1.00.

The Same. Large Paper Edition. 8vo. Tinted paper. $3.00.

Charles Sumner.

ORATIONS AND SPEECHES. 2 vols. $2.50.

RECENT SPEECHES AND ADDRESSES. $1.25.

John G. Whittier.

POCKET EDITION OF POETICAL WORKS. 2 vols. $1.50.

OLD PORTRAITS AND MODERN SKETCHES. 75 cents.

MARGARET SMITH'S JOURNAL. 75 cents.

SONGS OF LABOR, AND OTHER POEMS. Boards. 50 cts.

THE CHAPEL OF THE HERMITS. Cloth. 50 cents.

LITERARY RECREATIONS, &c. Cloth. $1.00.

THE PANORAMA, AND OTHER POEMS. Cloth. 50 cents.

Alexander Smith.

A LIFE DRAMA. 1 vol. 16mo. 50 cents.

CITY POEMS. With Portrait. 1 vol. 16mo. 63 cents.

Bayard Taylor.

POEMS OF HOME AND TRAVEL. Cloth. 75 cents.

POEMS OF THE ORIENT. Cloth. 75 cents.

Edwin P. Whipple.

ESSAYS AND REVIEWS. 2 vols. $2.00.

LECTURES ON LITERATURE AND LIFE. 63 cents.

WASHINGTON AND THE REVOLUTION. 20 cents.

Robert Browning.

Poetical Works. 2 vols. $2.00.
Men and Women. 1 vol. $1.00.

Henry Giles.

Lectures, Essays, &c. 2 vols. $1.50.
Discourses on Life. 75 cents.
Illustrations of Genius. Cloth. $1.00.

William Motherwell.

Complete Poetical Works. In Blue and Gold. 1 vol. 75 cents.
Minstrelsy, Anc. and Mod. 2 vols. Boards. $1.50.

Capt. Mayne Reid.

The Plant Hunters. With Plates. 75 cents.
The Desert Home: or, The Adventures of a Lost Family in the Wilderness. With fine Plates. $1.00.
The Boy Hunters. With fine Plates. 75 cents.
The Young Voyageurs: or, The Boy Hunters in the North. With Plates. 75 cents.
The Forest Exiles. With fine Plates. 75 cents.
The Bush Boys. With fine Plates. 75 cents.
The Young Yagers. With fine Plates. 75 cents.
Ran Away to Sea: An Autobiography for Boys. With fine Plates. 75 cents.
The Boy Tar: A Voyage in the Dark. A New Book. With fine Plates. 75 cents.

Goethe.

Wilhelm Meister. Translated by *Carlyle.* 2 vols. $2.50.
Faust. Translated by *Hayward.* 75 cents.
Faust. Translated by *Charles T. Brooks.* $1.00.
Correspondence with a Child. *Bettina.* 1 vol. 12mo. $1.25.

Rev. Charles Lowell.

PRACTICAL SERMONS. 1 vol. 12mo. $1.25.
OCCASIONAL SERMONS. With fine Portrait. $1.25.

Rev. F. W. Robertson.

SERMONS. First Series. $1.00.
" Second " $1.00.
" Third " $1.00.
" Fourth " $1.00.
LECTURES AND ADDRESSES ON LITERARY AND SOCIAL TOPICS. $1.00.

R. H. Stoddard.

POEMS. Cloth. 63 cents.
ADVENTURES IN FAIRY LAND. 75 cents.
SONGS OF SUMMER. 75 cents.

George Lunt.

LYRIC POEMS, &c. Cloth. 63 cents.
JULIA. A Poem. 50 cents.
THREE ERAS OF NEW ENGLAND. $1.00.

Philip James Bailey.

THE MYSTIC, AND OTHER POEMS. 50 cents.
THE ANGEL WORLD, &c. 50 cents.
THE AGE, A SATIRE. 75 cents.

Anna Mary Howitt.

AN ART STUDENT IN MUNICH. $1.25.
A SCHOOL OF LIFE. A Story. 75 cents.

Mary Russell Mitford.

OUR VILLAGE. Illustrated. 2 vols. 16mo. $2.50.
ATHERTON, AND OTHER STORIES. 1 vol. 16mo. $1.25.

Josiah Phillips Quincy.

LYTERIA: A DRAMATIC POEM. 50 cents.
CHARICLES: A DRAMATIC POEM. 50 cents.

Grace Greenwood.

GREENWOOD LEAVES. 1st and 2d Series. $1.25 each.
POETICAL WORKS. With fine Portrait. 75 cents.
HISTORY OF MY PETS. With six fine Engravings. Scarlet cloth. 50 cents.
RECOLLECTIONS OF MY CHILDHOOD. With six fine Engravings. Scarlet cloth. 50 cents.
HAPS AND MISHAPS OF A TOUR IN EUROPE. $1.25.
MERRIE ENGLAND. 75 cents.
A FOREST TRAGEDY, AND OTHER TALES. $1.00.
STORIES AND LEGENDS. 75 cents.
STORIES FROM FAMOUS BALLADS. Illustrated. 50 cents.

Mrs. Crosland.

LYDIA: A WOMAN'S BOOK. Cloth. 75 cents.
ENGLISH TALES AND SKETCHES. Cloth. $1.00.
MEMORABLE WOMEN. Illustrated. $1.00.

Mrs. Jameson.

CHARACTERISTICS OF WOMEN.	Blue and	Gold.	75 cents.
LOVES OF THE POETS.	"	"	75 cents.
DIARY OF AN ENNUYÉE	"	"	75 cents.
SKETCHES OF ART, &c.	"	"	75 cents.
STUDIES AND STORIES.	"	"	75 cents.
ITALIAN PAINTERS.	"	"	75 cents.

Mrs. Mowatt.

AUTOBIOGRAPHY OF AN ACTRESS. $1.25.
PLAYS. ARMAND AND FASHION. 50 cents.
MIMIC LIFE. 1 vol. $1.25.
THE TWIN ROSES. 1 vol. 75 cents.

Mrs. Howe.

PASSION FLOWERS. 75 cents.
WORDS FOR THE HOUR. 75 cents.
THE WORLD'S OWN. 50 cents.
A TRIP TO CUBA. 1 vol. 16mo. 75 cents.

Alice Cary.

POEMS. 1 vol. 16mo. $1.00.
CLOVERNOOK CHILDREN. With Plates. 75 cents.

Mrs. Eliza B. Lee.

MEMOIR OF THE BUCKMINSTERS. $1.25.
FLORENCE, THE PARISH ORPHAN. 50 cents.
PARTHENIA. 1 vol. 16mo. $1.00.

Samuel Smiles.

LIFE OF GEORGE STEPHENSON: ENGINEER. $1.00.
SELF HELP; WITH ILLUSTRATIONS OF CHARACTER AND CONDUCT. 1 vol. 75 cents.

Blanchard Jerrold.

DOUGLAS JERROLD'S WIT. 75 cents.
LIFE AND LETTERS OF DOUGLAS JERROLD. $1.00.

Trelawny.

RECOLLECTIONS OF SHELLEY AND BYRON. 75 cents.

Charles Sprague.

POETICAL AND PROSE WRITINGS. With fine Portrait. Boards. 75 cents.

Mrs. Lawrence.

LIGHT ON THE DARK RIVER: OR MEMOIRS OF MRS. HAMLIN. 1 vol. 16mo. Cloth. $1.00

Mrs. Judson.

Alderbrook. By *Fanny Forrester.* 2 vols. $1.75.

The Kathayan Slave, and Other Papers. 1 vol. 63 cents.

My Two Sisters: a Sketch from Memory. 50 cents.

G. A. Sala.

A Journey due North. $1.00.

Thomas W. Parsons.

Poems. $1.00.

John G. Saxe.

Poems. With Portrait. Boards. 63 cents. Cloth. 75 cents.

The Money King, and other Poems. 1 vol. 75 cents

Charles T. Brooks.

German Lyrics. Translated. 1 vol. 16mo. Cloth. $1.00.

Tom Brown.

School Days at Rugby. By *An Old Boy.* 1 vol. 16mo. $1.00.

The Same. Illustrated edition. $1.50.

The Scouring of the White Horse, or the Long Vacation Holiday of a London Clerk. By *The Author of 'School Days at Rugby.'* 1 vol. 16mo. $1.00.

Tom Brown at Oxford. A Sequel to School Days at Rugby. Parts I to IV. 12 cents each.

Leigh Hunt.

Poems. Blue and Gold. 2 vols. $1.50.

Gerald Massey.

Poetical Works. Blue and Gold. 75 cents.

C. W. Upham.

JOHN C. FREMONT'S LIFE, EXPLORATIONS, &c. With Illustrations. 75 cents.

W. M. Thackeray.

BALLADS. 1 vol. 16mo. 75 cents.

Charles Mackay.

POEMS. 1 vol. Cloth. $1.00.

George H. Boker.

PLAYS AND POEMS. 2 vols. $2.00.

Matthew Arnold.

POEMS. 75 cents.

Henry T. Tuckerman.

POEMS. Cloth. 75 cents.

James G. Percival.

POETICAL WORKS. 2 vols. Blue and Gold. $1.75.

Paul H. Hayne.

POEMS. 1 vol. 16mo. 63 cents.

AVOLIO, A LEGEND OF THE ISLAND OF COS; AND OTHER POEMS. 1 vol. 75 cents.

Mrs. A. C. Lowell.

SEED-GRAIN FOR THOUGHT AND DISCUSSION. 2 vols. $1.75.

EDUCATION OF GIRLS. 25 cents.

G. H. Lewes.

The Life and Works of Goethe. 2 vols. 16mo. $2.50.

Washington Allston.

Monaldi, a Tale. 1 vol. 16mo. 75 cents.

Arthur P. Stanley.

Life and Correspondence of Dr. Arnold. 2 vols. $2.00.

Henry Kingsley.

Recollections of Geoffry Hamlyn. A Novel. $1.25.

Dr. John C. Warren.

The Preservation of Health, &c. 1 vol. 38 cents.

Life. By Edward Warren, M. D. Compiled chiefly from his Private Journals. 2 vols. 8vo. $3.50.

Joseph T. Buckingham.

Personal Memoirs and Recollections of Editorial Life. With Portrait. 2 vols. 16mo. $1.50.

Theophilus Parsons.

A Memoir of Chief Justice Theophilus Parsons, with Notices of some of his Contemporaries. By his Son. With Portrait. 1 vol. 12mo. $1.50.

Goldsmith.

The Vicar of Wakefield. Illustrated Edition. $3.00.

Horace Mann.

Thoughts for a Young Man. 25 cents.

Dr. William E. Coale.

HINTS ON HEALTH. 3d Edition. 63 cents.

Lord Dufferin.

A YACHT VOYAGE OF 6,000 MILES. $1.00.

Fanny Kemble.

POEMS. Enlarged Edition. $1.00.

Owen Meredith.

POETICAL WORKS. Blue and Gold. 75 cents.

Arago.

BIOGRAPHIES OF DISTINGUISHED SCIENTIFIC MEN. 16mo. 2 vols. $2.00.

R. H. Dana, Jr.

TO CUBA AND BACK, a Vacation Voyage, by the Author of "Two Years before the Mast." 75 cents.

John Neal.

TRUE WOMANHOOD. A Novel. 1 vol. $1.25.

Julia Kavanagh.

SEVEN YEARS. A VOLUME OF STORIES. 8vo. Paper. 30 cents.

G. J. Whyte Melville.

HOLMBY HOUSE: A TALE OF OLD NORTHAMPTONSHIRE. 8vo. Paper.

Captain McClintock.

Narrative of the Voyage in search of Sir John Franklin and the Discovery of his Remains. With Maps and Illustrations. 1 vol. large 12mo. $1.50.

Charles Eliot Norton.

Notes of Travel and Study in Italy. 1 vol. 16mo. $1.00. *Just ready.*

Poems. By Miss Muloch, Author of "John Halifax," &c. 1 vol. 75 cents.

Poems. By Sydney Dobell. 1 vol. Blue and Gold. 75 cts.

Arabian Days' Entertainments. Translated from the German of W. Hauff. By H. Pelham Curtis. With Illustrations by Hoppin. 1 vol. $1.25.

Hymns of the Ages. With a Preface by Rev. F. D. Huntington, D. D. 1 vol. 12mo. $1.00.

Also a fine Edition, on large paper. 8vo. Bevelled boards. $3.00.

The Crusades and the Crusaders. By J. G. Edgar. With Illustrations. 75 cents.

Ernest Bracebridge; or, Schoolboy Days. By W. H. G. Kingston. With Illustrations. 75 cents.

Poems. By Henry Timrod. 1 vol. 16mo. 50 cents.

Sword and Gown. By the Author of "Guy Livingstone." 1 vol. 75 cents.

Almost a Heroine. By the Author of "Charles Auchester," and "Counterparts." 1 vol. $1.00.

Twelve Years of a Soldier's Life: A Memoir of the Late Major W. S. R. Hodson, B. A. Edited by his Brother, Rev. George H. Hodson. 1 vol. $1.00.

Rab and his Friends. By John Brown, M. D. 15 cents.

The Life and Times of Sir Philip Sidney. 1 vol. 16mo. $1.00.

Ernest Carroll, or Artist Life in Italy. 1 vol. 16mo. 88 cents.

Christmas Hours. By the Author of "The Homeward Path," &c. 1 vol. 16mo. 50 cents.

Memory and Hope. Cloth. $2.00.

THALATTA; A BOOK FOR THE SEASIDE. 75 cents.

REJECTED ADDRESSES. A new edition. Cloth. 75 cents.

WARRENIANA; A COMPANION TO REJECTED ADDRESSES. 63 cents.

ANGEL VOICES. 38 cents.

THE BOSTON BOOK. $1.25.

MEMOIR OF ROBERT WHEATON. 1 vol. $1.00.

LABOR AND LOVE: A TALE OF ENGLISH LIFE. 50 cts.

THE SOLITARY OF JUAN FERNANDEZ. By the Author of Picciola. 50 cents.

WALDEN: OR, LIFE IN THE WOODS. By Henry D. Thoreau. 1 vol. 16mo. $1.00.

VILLAGE LIFE IN EGYPT. By Bayle St. John, the Author of "Purple Tints of Paris." 2 vols. 16mo. $1.25.

WENSLEY: A STORY WITHOUT A MORAL. By Edmund Quincy. 75 cents.

PALISSY THE POTTER. By Henry Morley. 2 vols. 16mo. $1.50.

THE BARCLAYS OF BOSTON. By Mrs. H. G. Otis. 1 vol. 12mo. $1.25.

SIR ROGER DE COVERLEY. By Addison. From the "Spectator." 75 cents.

SERMONS OF CONSOLATION. By F. W. P. Greenwood. $1.00.

SPAIN, HER INSTITUTIONS, POLITICS, AND PUBLIC MEN. By S. T. Wallis. $1.00.

POEMS. By Henry Alford. $1.25.

ESSAYS ON THE FORMATION OF OPINIONS AND THE PURSUIT OF TRUTH. By Samuel Bailey. 1 vol. 16mo. $1.00.

POEMS OF MANY YEARS. By Richard Monckton Milnes. Boards. 75 cents.

BOTHWELL. By W. Edmondstoune Aytoun. 75 cents.

POEMS. By Mrs. Rosa V. Johnson. 1 vol. 16mo. $1.00.

THORPE: A QUIET ENGLISH TOWN, AND HUMAN LIFE THEREIN. By William Mountford. 16mo. $1.00

MATINS AND VESPERS. By John Bowring. Blue and Gold. 75 cents.

OAKFIELD. A Novel. By Lieut. Arnold. $1.00.

LECTURES ON ORATORY AND RHETORIC. By Prof. E. T. Channing. 75 cents.

A PHYSICIAN'S VACATION. By Dr. Walter Channing. $1.50.

A PHYSIOLOGICAL COOKERY BOOK. By Mrs. Horace Mann. 63 cents.

WILLIAM WORDSWORTH'S BIOGRAPHY. By Christopher Wosrdworth. 2 vols. $2.50.

NOTES FROM LIFE. By the Author of "Philip Van Artevelde." 1 vol. 16mo. Cloth. 63 cents.

ART OF PROLONGING LIFE. By Hufeland. Edited by Erasmus Wilson. 1 vol. 16mo. 75 cents.

SHELLEY MEMORIALS. From Authentic Sources. 1 vol. Cloth. 75 cents.

POEMS AND PARODIES. By Phœbe Cary. 75 cents.

LIFE OF EDMUND BURKE. By James Prior. 2 vols. $2.00.

CHURCH AND CONGREGATION. By C. A. Bartol. $1.00.

THORNDALE, OR THE CONFLICT OF OPINIONS. By William Smith. $1.25.

In Blue and Gold.

LONGFELLOW'S POETICAL WORKS. 2 vols. $1.75.
do. PROSE WORKS. 2 vols. $1.75.
TENNYSON'S POETICAL WORKS. 1 vol. 75 cents.
WHITTIER'S POETICAL WORKS. 2 vols. $1.50.
LEIGH HUNT'S POETICAL WORKS. 2 vols. $1.50.
GERALD MASSEY'S POETICAL WORKS. 1 vol. 75 cents.
MRS. JAMESON'S CHARACTERISTICS OF WOMEN. 75 cts.
do. DIARY OF AN ENNUYÉE. 1 vol. 75 cts.
do. LOVES OF THE POETS. 1 vol. 75 cts.
do. SKETCHES OF ART, &c. 1 vol. 75 cts.
do. STUDIES AND STORIES. 1 vol. 75 cts.
do. ITALIAN PAINTERS. 1 vol. 75 cents.
OWEN MEREDITH'S POEMS. 1 vol. 75 cents.
BOWRING'S MATINS AND VESPERS. 1 vol. 75 cents.
LOWELL'S (J. RUSSELL) POETICAL WORKS. 2 vols. $1.50.
PERCIVAL'S POETICAL WORKS. 2 vols. $1.75.
MOTHERWELL'S POEMS. 1 vol. 75 cents.
SYDNEY DOBELL'S POEMS. 1 vol. 75 cents.

www.ingramcontent.com/pod-product-compliance
Lightning Source LLC
LaVergne TN
LVHW021408110826
845150LV00007B/1841